"To all who continually inspire me - Thank You"

Best Wishes,

Valerie

"Knowing how to think properly is an obvious and essential skill if you want to stay one step ahead of the pack in business. The mystery is that so few people invest in their thinking skills.

*Most of us assume that we do – until we meet someone like Valerie Pierce, creator of the **Clear and Critical Thinking** programmes. An afternoon with Pierce will leave you feeling that you have woken out of a coma."*

Tina-Marie O'Neill, journalist, Business Post

ISBN: 978-1-916620-23-0

AUTHOR
Valerie Pierce
www.clearthinkinginaction.com

BOOK DESIGN
Anouk Denoyelle

BOOK COVER
Lauren Grant

PRINTED BY
Lettertec
www.lettertec.com

Printed in the EU

Content

Introduction ↗

Dear Reader,

Thank you for taking up this book and I hope you will enjoy the short story you are about to encounter.

My name is Valerie and I am a philosopher by trade. Over 20 years ago I created training courses on how to develop our **'Clear & Critical Thinking'** skills, to be clever when we want to be, so as to achieve what we want, when we want it.

My interest is in how we behave in situations we believe are difficult and which frustrate us so we don't or can't reach our goals. My goal is to ensure that you overcome this frustration, this inability to overcome the negative thinking that blocks your progress.

My aim is to help you to transform your negative thinking into positive and innovative action.

In other words – MAKE THE 'NO' DAY A YESTERDAY.

MAKE THE 'NO' DAY A YESTERDAY

as illustrated
in the bag story →

FROM	TO	DATE	TIME	PASSENGER
Dublin	**London**	**25 Jun**	**7:30 PM**	**1 pers**

"Have you ever arrived at an airport and your bag didn't?"

I know. It's an awful experience, standing there at the conveyor belt thingie, seeing all the other bags rolling along, heart sinking, anger mounting, hysteria beginning to show.

I think to myself, "This can't be happening...I have a really important gig – speaking at a conference for a very prestigious firm...all the papers, all the clothes I need are in that bag. Please God, I have to have that bag..."

Still no sign. The conveyor belt rolls on. Other people smile, picking up their beloved bags...What do I do? It's now 7.30pm. Getting late to find help.

"Think, Valerie. You need to find someone to help".

The airline woman walks confidently over to me. She smiles sympathetically...She is very sympathetic.

You might think this is a very good thing, but in fact, it is a very bad thing. Although sympathy might feel good, in thinking terms, sympathy means 'NO'.

When somebody is sympathetic to you, it means you are NOT going to get what you want; that is why they are being sympathetic…

**"I'm so sorry, Madam,
this is such an awful situation for you."**

=

You're not getting your bag tonight.

So I say, *"Please, you must stop the sympathy because I really need the bag"*. She then turns to realism…This is the same message as sympathy, but tougher. It means get a grip…you are not getting your bag.

"We have to be realistic," she says, *"It's impossible to recover your bag tonight"*. She has the power, and all the cards, the wall of negativity seems insurmountable. Though, *"hold on"*, I think, maybe the clue to solving my problem is in her negative realism…

"What do you mean when you say we have to be realistic? I say. *"Why do you think we cannot get this bag this evening".*

She looks very comfortable, basking in the knowledge of the reasons why she CANNOT get my bag.

"It's very simple Madam", she says.

01 The offices in Dublin are closed

02 We have no more carriers this evening

03 We have a 'no same day' policy

(This last and third reason is quite bizarre, I know...Some 24hr cover for the airline to ensure they have at least 24 hours to return your lost property).

"Therefore", she said, *"you see, we cannot get your bag this evening"*.

This logic is compelling. Its seduction lies in the fact that these ideas seem impossible to overcome, and therefore, we believe we cannot solve the problem.

At this point, most people change to 'creative thinking'. The airline employee did in this case also, as suddenly, with a glimmer of glee, she continues – *"so let's see if we can solve your problem another way. You need clothes, so let's see what we can find in the airport shops, and can we not receive your papers for your conference another way? Can they be emailed over to us?"*.

Well, I was amazed. She had some good ideas to solve my situation, I thought she most definitely was on a very good 'Dealing with Difficult Customers' Training Course recently.

And I almost went with these suggestions, as they really made sense. That was the problem, this whole thing made sense. The airline woman was so persuasive, her logic made complete sense - I could not have my bag that night - Everyone could see that. I was doomed to go with her creativity...

Then it dawned on me...We were focused on all the reasons why I couldn't get my bag.

But why not turn these around to see if they could tell us HOW to get my bag?

I know this sounds crazy, and I was desperate. But think about it. If these are the reasons why I cannot get my bag – 'no, because' etc...

Why can we not overcome these to give us a 'yes if'...?

NO BECAUSE $=$ YES, IF...

Let's see how that looks...

NO, I CANNOT get my bag BECAUSE the offices are closed, there are no more carriers this evening and there is a 'no same day' policy.

means...

YES, I can get my bag IF...

| 01 | we get an open office in Dublin |
| 02 we get a carrier this evening | 03 we overcome the 'same day policy' |

So, my answer is simple. In working through the very negatives I think are STOPPING me from getting what I want, amazingly, I can get exactly what I need.

That is, if we can stop being seduced by the logic that is persuading us we cannot do something. If we can overcome the emotional turmoil this impasse is creating in our thinking, then we can use these negative thoughts to stimulate our imagination.

Using negative thinking to stimulate our imagination changes negative thoughts into our most powerful form of intelligence. Therefore, negative thoughts can get things done. It is all down to the way we use them.

So, returning to my bag story, some instinct made me believe we could tackle the first negative – 'the closed offices in Dublin'. I meekly suggested to the airline woman, that if we couldn't get the bag because the offices in Dublin were closed, then was it possible that we might be able to retrieve the bag, if we could find an OPEN office?

She thought that possible, so I asked her for the phone numbers of some offices in Dublin and found there were two. We telephoned one of them and what do you think happened? Somebody answered the phone...the office was OPEN.

The big lesson here is never to confuse logic with the truth...

She assumed the office was closed, but in truth, it was not. However, her brilliance was now going to swing into action because her negativity was based on her knowledge of what she needed. She needed an open office to source the bag, retag it, and put it back into the system.

So once we had the open office, off she went, resourced the bag, retagged the bag and put it back into the system.

BLOCK No.1 OVERCOME ✓

Once the bag was in the system, the operatives in Dublin put it onto a different airline carrier. We have many going from Dublin to London and this was a very simple negative to deal with.

BLOCK No.2 OVERCOME ✓

But let me tell you the most amazing thing of all. When the bag arrived at the airport in London, my lovely airline lady just simply ignored the 'same day' policy, which made absolutely no sense now, and put the bag into a taxi, and on its way to my hotel.

BLOCK No.3 OVERCOME ✓

I received my bag that night at 11.00pm.

What do you think happened to achieve this success? Let's analyse the situation so that we can create a successful methodology.

We have a very negative situation, one that seems insurmountable. The negative thought process is being used as a BARRIER to progression because it is a thought process that is seducing and persuading us that our goal is impossible. But this is only a thought process...Once we changed our thinking, and used these negatives thoughts as a SIGNPOST to achieve the goal, we realised that we could produce the ideas needed to reach our ideal.

So why am I telling you this experience I had at the airport many years ago. It is a simple story where when I finally retrieved my bag, I felt very relieved. I wanted nothing more than to forget the whole incident. But the company running the conference insisted I tell this story at their conference the next day. They explained that the worst problem they had in their organisation was their people being seduced by these barriers thrown up by negative thinking.

In their business organisation, when they wanted to try a new idea or create a new system, they were always blocked by their negative thoughts. They were always a huge hurdle to overcome, causing stress in the workplace. The management team felt that if their people could see that negative thoughts were the answer to all their problems, then their work would be so much easier.

And that is why reader, I am writing this to you today. A very simple story can tell us so much about how we can tackle our everyday problems.

I use this methodology now all the time and I suggest you do too the next time you want to do something you feel is too difficult, or even impossible.

WHY NOT = HOW TO

I suggest you write down all the reasons WHY YOU CANNOT do what you wish. For instance "no time", "not enough money".

Now look at these reasons, they are your brilliant form of intelligence telling you 'HOW TO' do exactly what you wish. They are telling you get the time, get the money and you have exactly what you want.

Exercises

So let's get this working for you, I would like you to create your own story of success. Your negative thoughts are of so much more value if you can use them to stimulate your imagination – they can take you anywhere you want to go...

Exercise 1:

Some questions to help you get started.

▶ What does 'No, because = Yes, if' mean to you?

▶ What words feel better for you....what words would come to mind for you when you are in a negative situation?

Exercise 2:
What you can learn from your past experience.

▶ What do you think would give you the confidence to change your negative thinking into positive action?

Exercise 3:
Be Innovative.

▸ Can you think of a negative situation you have encountered recently and how you dealt with that situation?

▸ Even if you weren't able to overcome those negatives, what ideas do you think you can produce now to reach your longed for ideal....?

Exercise 4:
Now write your own success story.

▸ Think of a goal you want to achieve. Now write down all the reasons why your CANNOT achieve your goal.

▸ Rank these negatives from the easiest to solve first down to the most difficult.

▸ One by one, let your imagination free to create ideas to overcome these negatives.

▸ Implement your ideas into action.

Reference list
of illustrations ↘

Page 14

Freepik. Download, July 2nd, 2023. www.freepik.com, vector illustration airplane 13164923. Composition by Anouk Denoyelle.

Freepik. Download, July 2nd, 2023. www.freepik.com, vector illustration London 3150955. Composition by Anouk Denoyelle.

Freepik. Download, July 8th, 2023. www.freepik.com, vector illustration bags 13031414. Composition by Anouk Denoyelle.

Page 20

Freepik. Download, July 15th, 2023. www.freepik.com, vector illustration document 10762770. Composition by Anouk Denoyelle.

Freepik. Download, July 27th, 2023. www.freepik.com, vector illustration envelop 5777076. Composition by Anouk Denoyelle.

Freepik. Download, July 18th, 2023. www.freepik.com, vector illustration light bulb 20289401. Composition by Anouk Denoyelle.

Freepik. Download, July 20th, 2023. www.freepik.com, vector illustration coffee cup 1577128. Composition by Anouk Denoyelle.

Page 27

Freepik. Download, July 3rd, 2023. www.freepik.com, vector illustration open sign 8356515. Composition by Anouk Denoyelle.

Freepik. Download, July 18th, 2023. www.freepik.com, vector illustration telephon 20148397. Composition by Anouk Denoyelle.

Freepik. Download, July 21st, 2023. www.freepik.com, vector illustration suitcase 13031413. Composition by Anouk Denoyelle.

Freepik. Download, July 25th, 2023. www.freepik.com, vector illustration clover leaves 7186087. Composition by Anouk Denoyelle.

Page 28

Freepik. Download, July 9th, 2023. www.freepik.com, vector illustration airplane 6146035. Composition by Anouk Denoyelle.

Freepik. Download, July 11th, 2023. www.freepik.com, vector illustration suitcase 33238998. Composition by Anouk Denoyelle.

Freepik. Download, August 1st, 2023. www.freepik.com, vector illustration building 2448781. Composition by Anouk Denoyelle.

Page 31

Freepik. Download, July 23th, 2023. www.freepik.com, vector illustration target 4407286. Composition by Anouk Denoyelle.

Freepik. Download, July 16th, 2023. www.freepik.com, vector illustration confusion 17294084. Composition by Anouk Denoyelle.

Freepik. Download, August 3rd, 2023. www.freepik.com, vector illustration signposts 13381592. Composition by Anouk Denoyelle.

VALERIE PIERCE
International

3 The Square, Beggars Bush,
Ballsbridge Dublin, D04 HC52, Ireland

M +353 87 225 2889

E vpierce@clearthinkinginaction.com
W www.clearthinkinginaction.com